Psychotic

Poems by
Shannon Fabre

Cover Art by
Valena

Shannon Fabre
Psychotic

MLMC–Gothic and Main
Northampton, MA

Published by MLMC–Gothic and Main
29 Butler Place, #2
Northampton, MA 01060
http://www.mlmc-media.com

Cover art by Valena
Gothic and Main logo by Renetta Hood.

ISBN 978-1-63328-010-6

TABLE OF CONTENTS

This book is dedicated to my mother, Krista Shields-Lewis, who always believed in me and never abandoned me. It is also for my grandmother, Georgia Fabre-Peltier, who instilled in me a love of reading and poetry.

Hello

Hello out there, from this altered actuality.
I must have written a hundred lines
To tell you I'm sorry that I went absentee.

Last we spoke you said with brutality,
"Don't call. I've heard all your lines."
Talking to you is a lesson in finality.

Hello out there from this demented hyperbole.
I wrote you a hundred lines already.
My messages reveal a break-up with reality.

Psychotic

I went to the priest to give my confession.
I told him I felt as if under hypnosis.
He answered I suffered demonic obsession,
A somewhat confounding surprise diagnosis.

I went to another, for modern-day gnosis.
He gladly proclaimed post-partum depression.
His worldly advice a depressing prognosis,
But wholly congruous with his sole profession.

But I was divided: had I seen the devil?
The collared man said it was all diabolic,
And dastardly thoughts seemed in me to revel,
Fueled on by what science had deemed metabolic.

All three of these men I examined eye level:
Despite the road taken, I end up melancholic.
Three paths in the woods and all left me bedeviled,
With a newly found relish of thoughts hyberbolic.

Advice

When love is a feeling as light as a feather,
Be wary of falling into the darkest abyss
If the air is cool with Spring-like weather.

When love flows freely like an azure river,
Be wary of the fluid embrace and the kiss
If engulfing pleasure sets your soul to shiver.

When seat covers smell like polished leather
It is always best to refuse, repel, and resist
If the speed of his love you've yet to measure.

When meandering glances cause eyes to align,
It is prudent to slither away with snake-like hiss
When the truth of his love you have yet to divine.

Hell

Hell is an ignorant, intrepid priest.
He says what I see makes me a true seer,
A vaticanized superstitious scholar at least.
Says there is a certain whisper only I can hear,
A sickly sweet tune by an unknown bard,
A devilish ear-ringing that will not cease.

Hell is family that is super-superstitious.
Their delusions, they soon believe to be real,
Their actions pernicious, at least injudicious.
Hell is angelic minions real in their zeal,
They strapped me and rolled me to the psycho ward.
Unforgivable they still are, but at least expeditious.

Julia

Julia walked slowly, her head hung down low.
The nurse brought cheap shampoo for our ablutions;
It turned my flowing hair into a giant, twisted knot.
Julia combed it slowly, but it often still got caught
And in her nimble fingers it would be ensnared,
But she tugged at it gently so it would stay strong.
By the time I went home it was silken and plush.

The death of her child was a terrible blow.
So seeds of suicide bloomed, a pretty solution.
She said she was sorry that she had been stopped;
With me in the psych ward she now lived distraught.
One day I asked Julia to share, her most sacred prayer:
She said the life of a star is one for which she longed.
We laughed, looked at TV, and drank our orange crush.

Colors

Certain colors have the power to remind me of you,
Like the black of my dress with the lacy accent—
Though now when I wear it, it makes me quite blue.
You'd lie in my gold sheets, your eyes discontent,
Modest Mouse in the background, a world a bit askew.

I think of tan freckled hands as they stroked my hair,
Your sun-reddened shoulders, a sight once commonplace.
How white I turned when you dissolved in thin air.
How quickly color drained from your dear mother's face,
When I told her I was pregnant, with a fixed, green-eyed stare.

Marigolds and Mums

Marigolds and mums are today in their bloom;
They foretell the arrival of my darkest of seasons,
Held captive by drizzle and two guards in my room:
Delusion and Disorder did not give their reasons.
I loom at the window, bird of my own doom.

The wind in winter flexes and shows off its power,
And no yellow or orange panorama I'll find.
The barren, dead landscape makes me feel dour,
And the whiteness renders me colorless, blind.
But marigolds and mums mark my darkest of hours.

Wild Gypsy Eyes

"Don't you want to get lost in my wild gypsy eyes?
I'll dress to the nines, in my wild dancing clothes.
Though a Pandora's box, I'm still quite a prize—
The longer you look, your devotion will grow.
My wildly forked tongue licks a lip full of lies,
But my song will disguise that my dance is a pose."

Wild-clad but naïve, I'm the partner he chose,
But he missed a step, and his face dropped its guise.
Now a fickle-eyed child with half-gypsy blood grows
Through her fatherless days, her life filled with cries—
Her agonized notes were the song he composed,
And her once dancing mother must freeze, paralyzed.

Doom and Gloom

I waited for you for 100 years.
Locked in the prison that was you,
I cried more than 1000 tears.

You played on my worst fears.
When I just wanted to say "I do,"
You wanted only smokes and beer.

Now I am shadowed by gloom.
I go a little crazy each spring,
When darkness arises to fill my room.

Somehow I missed the messages of doom.
When you said it was only a fling.
Over each happiness shadows now loom.

Gypsy Kiss

He gave me a gypsy kiss.
A kiss I knew I would soon miss.
It smelled like rose essence,
I was in evanescent, ethereal bliss.
Now of his blond curls I reminisce.
He had asked, I acquiesced.

I knew all along he was leaving,
Soon to engage in some minor thieving.
I thought he would return to me, maybe.
But my heart was left infinitely grieving,
My frame shaking hard from the heaving.
And my body sheltering a gypsy baby.

Lost But Found

Left holding dead spring flowers, I lost you to cocaine.
In my summer dress I said the words; I lost you once again.
From the depths of my depression, I watched you take a fall
Your heart a winter landscape, your succor a pub crawl.

When I finally chanced upon you, right through you I could see.
But your presence left me pregnant, with no pot in which to pee.
Now I'm unphazed by your vanishing, but I find I must abstain
From wishing you the curse of needing hair-plugs and Rogaine.

I'm looking forward to the time our child will want to know
About post-partum sorrow and her mother's near-death woe.
She'll learn her mother's sacrifice, her father's altered truths,
And his magic act that starred a champagne glass and gran's vermouth.

Manic Depression

I'm a manic maniac but downtrodden, delusional, depressive,
My world is inside out, bright red stained a gray hue,
I think I am in Jackson Square while at Audubon Zoo,
But feel tethered to the bed because my soul is blue,
I buzz brazenly and boldly, a queen bee protecting precious honey,
Or wear polka dots predominantly, and paisley proudly.
And my very presence is so loud that people stare
If I wear old yoga pants, don't brush my teeth, or hair,
Or lie on the couch and find nothing and no one funny,
Or wonder why friends come and go, their travels my trials,
As though all the world is wonderful, or even slightly fair.

Undone

I'm quite afraid that I came completely undone
When I told you all about the baby.
I thought that we burned the midnight sun.
I thought that you were the one, well maybe.
It turns out I just relived a rerun.

With dirty bathwater some mop the floor,
But I hate reasons cloaked in obfuscation.
It was the same old scene I'd seen before:
Man leaves baby girl despite protestation.
My own Daddy threw me out the door.

Crooked Church

The church we liked was falling down.
Its edifice crooked; I thought it an omen:
Maybe our love was destined to drown.

In tears I confided; you played the clown—
Before I showed, you were quite the showman,
But that church's facade became God's frown.

I thought the church would be love's home,
But the crooked church collapsed; departing, we parted.
The rains came and filled the fallen dome.

Burning Candles

I burned some candles just for you.
Placed carefully inside my kitchen windows,
Flickering brightly, St. Anthony's white hues.

They glowed like torches, illuminating my view.
In that kitchen I danced with eerie shadows,
But shadow play caused my vision to skew.

For things long lost I said Novena.
You are misplaced, out somewhere, drinking.
We sit at the kitchen table, eating Farina.

I prayed for intersession, dear Magdalena.
I said for your life I was wrought with fear—
But you could not hear from your carnal cantina.

Before Bi-Polar

She paces and paces, up and down the hall,
Chain smoking Pal-Mals and biting hang nails,
She feels. She cries. She tries. She fails.
Again the meds slam her up against the wall.
She has to watch her step so she won't fall,
And cover up her ears to the suicidal wails.

Before each slight sound became a strong gale,
Before diagnosis became her coffin nail,
Her talents brought many a warm curtain call.
On a bleak prognosis her song was impaled.
And now she is careful when telling the tale
Of a previous life, when she felt ten feet tall.

The Narrow Gauge

The train lurched, creaked forward and rattled.
My paranoia was by this circumstance amplified.
Hidden from others, with my sanity I grappled.
The disquiet I felt in my soul was intensified,
Below, the dangerous Animas River awaited.

Up the slope, up the Narrow Gauge we battled.
Steam falling into the abyss—my soul personified.
Others aboard sat chatting and smiling; I was addled.
The engines rumbling in my mind was magnified.
The forceful Animas River would not be subjugated.

Five hundred feet below the trestles descended.
Time stood still as we slowed to a dead stop;
We revved up again and we turned as intended.
We rolled to the station, graced by its gift shop.
The beautiful Animas River flowed on unabated.

Saint Jude

Oh thou glorified patron saint of impossible causes,
I wonder what you would think of me,
My cause in obscurity; my world in mirages.

I visit New Orleans, a vibrant variety of plazas,
Hoping the saints were near, but I saw them flee.
I thought about history, stopped for brief pauses.

And found myself moving faster, the devil in view.
I sped away to St. Louis Cathedral, my sanctuary.
That clever devil saw me through the stained glass hue,

Backed to a corner, I grabbed his tail till he knew
He'd met a worthy—or at least adequate—adversary.
I dusted my hands, made my way to a back row pew.

The Angel on the Corner

It was a harvest moon, Halloween night,
I walked forty two blocks from the quarter.
Passed the By-water barefoot; felt fear at my plight.
I wished for even one single, solitary supporter—
Saw only the crack of early morning light.

I was on Dauphine, just past Piety.
A random old man said I looked harrowed.
Breakfast he offered—I accepted with anxiety.
Down a hall narrowed, into a room hallowed,
His aura a halo that glowed with sobriety.

Cloud Watching

Together we read *The Wind in the Willows*.
Together we pretended to fight with pillows.
Together we watched a giant cloud billow.
"Two giant armadillos," you'd proudly report,
With your little laugh as the clouds contort.
To think your father wanted to abort.

Queen of Hearts

On absolute truth I most desperately insisted,
Questions straightforward; avowals corrupted.
And when offered an exit, you firmly insisted;
My bete noir devil, your mind games persisted.

But you were the rogue resolute at my threshold.
One kiss my soul bought and made me your strumpet.
Polite conversation had no chance for a foothold.
When I played the jilted, you claimed it was foretold.

A mere novice I was, the fabled Queen of Hearts,
Aligning the charts, although I was their puppet.
Ever the changeling, the wise fool was your part
In a King of Swords guise you'd strike and depart.

Knocked Up in Louisiana

A Cajun father, his daughter knocked up
Doesn't show any anger. He just doesn't speak.
Nothing he says when he throws coffee cups.
And wordless his slap, when he strikes her cheek.

For lesser infractions her Mother he would beat.
She now misses her my family, misses fine cuisine,
But does not think leaving the slightest defeat—
She found many like her, and dark roasted beans.

Jillian Believes

Jillian believes in a justified, Jesuit, Jahweh Jesus.
She also believes in the power of evil.
Jillian thinks the former has the power to free us.
Of the latter, everything we do, well he sees us.

Jillian believes he creeps right in, this reprobate.
She thinks that the price was high and pre-paid
At the cross with thorn-crown fashioned from hate
And large spiked nails. On this she would cogitate.

Jillian forgets that the devil once to me conveyed
(Either it was he or a figment of my psyche)
That it made little difference how often I prayed,
My sentence a macabre, morbid hell, because I strayed.

That Old Jagged Cross

The jagged little cross she now must bear
She knows will never, ever go away.
Her nails made sure through her skin to tear.

The jagged little cross, well it just isn't fair.
She once created it while led astray,
But permanent scars are the fashion she wears.

One jagged little cross across her chest.
And to think self-mutilation was never her thing—
But with the gift of the jagged cross she was blessed.

Exorcizing Demons

To exorcize a fiend two camps thus align:
Toward the supernatural explanation
Some are invariably, inexorably inclined—
Hence the oldest way, the rite of exorcism;

But some thought that due to my condition
"Demon" was a word too trite and benign.
How one could be real, but still an apparition?
His tousled blonde hair was quite serpentine.

Lechery and Debauchery

Your dreams were devilish debauchery.
I was no libertine, not free, but able to see
Through your mockery, filth, lechery.

But you loved me in my girlish pink dress
(Though I suppose you loved me a good bit less)
And gave me a pink child with such largesse.

An irreconcilable mess, heart stuck in the mire,
Though what survived was some kind of desire,
Futile and unrequited. My love for you expired.

Dear Prudence

When you were little, you adored me.
You learned to ride a bike at four.
I thought you were a prodigy
That no one else could see.

In the first grade you tried to flee.
The systematic, cyclic abuse unseen,
A revolving door, your Father's house.
It was his excuse to curse, demean.

Debaser, demoralizer, you know what he is.
But now you wear your sex on your sleeve
Like a cheap button. Your brain became a schiz.
You're an adult who is defined by simply being his.

Dysfunctional

She thought you were big, thought you tall
When she was told you went on safari in Africa.
When you left for your trip she was too small.
But then at night for you she would bawl.
Left with Grandma who still believed in Fatima.
As for you, you never had the decency to call.

Now that she's older, she feel the effects
Whether rightfully so—or not. She feels rejected
By all. She knows they notice her defects.
Her relationships with men tend to be complex—
A collection of exes. But it's you she's projected.
And they can't understand. They say she perplexes.

Dysfunctional, Part Two

You owe her brother, sister and her—and their mothers—an apology,
But an apology is what they are unlikely to ever hear or see.
What they never knew they'd get was a lesson in psychology.

You totally and completely missed the Church's catechism on pathology.
You were ruthless, and you made them for their very lives plea—
I still don't fully understand the nature of your demented ideology.

Your father—beat their Grandmother. So the twisted, diabolic cycle began.
Your life has been rotten, rife with violence, hypocrisy, misogyny….
A life you spent at home—but with a joint and a beer can.

The First Snow in November

The first snow in November was when we met
Under the evanescent light I danced on the moon.
I didn't know I was working without a net.

The first snow in November, and the sky all in cloud
Void of child-like shapes, just the drizzling rain and snow,
We were alone, but you lost me in a crowd.

The first snow in November, and your face in shroud,
The white between us just seemed to grow and grow,
I called out your name, the wind must have been too loud.

The first snow in November, alone, cold, and wet.
I watch the ground turn into white space, drifting dunes,
But with blankets and layers, I think I'll be set.

Xanax and Lithium

The bitter taste in the back of my throat
I have learned will each day be the same.
In a weird, wayward world I aimlessly float
A drifting existence, no place to lay blame
Life on a vast ocean without a lifeboat.

My friends tell me that I should try pot,
But tremors are better than munchies by far.
A wandering peace of mind can be bought:
The muddled effects just are what they are.
For this small bit of sanity I have fought.

The Bridge You Burned

Most days you can find me on the porch sipping tea
Lost in fond reveries of the bridge you set ablaze.
You bought the incendiary; I was billed the fee.
I'm toasty now, shiver-free from your icy touches.
Little I care if the wind gusts straight or shifts sideways—
And my once pallid cheeks have new warm, softer blushes.

Twisted

You dangled your love like a gem high above me.
You tangled my mind with each truth that you yanked.
Contorted, I twisted, caught up on your spindle tree;
I jangled as agitated bracelets chimed in and clanked.
You lorded above your subject, a self-anointed king
Who distorted love and recreated me as plaything.

Acrid your attitude, vile, disloyal, common, and petty,
Keeping me in servitude with heavy chains of affection.
Dollish were my dresses, but you offered wine so heady
That slow was my certitude, perplexed without direction.
To abolish your power I looked hard through your finery,
Demolished those chains, and found the finest winery.

Cheating the Reaper

I have spent one hundred seasons in hell.
Your proclivity for opium became my bane;
Your valuing valium made my love vain.
From your corrupt well, I drank gin and sin.

For purple poppies you'd sell your own skin.
Your future demise is my present-day pain.
You forged your feelings; love became profane.
My soul was starved on the wax fruit that fell.

And you thought me murdered; I merely bled
From your silent scythe. My recycle was blissful.
Now newly sown seed, my rebirth will be mindful
That nature's frenzy sometimes reboots the dead.

The Corporal's Corpse

A cynical coalition conceded, "the corporal was flotsam."
After he washed ashore he was loaded into the Boeing.
His last pilot pondered the too-high price of petroleum.
The laudanum-laden mortician prepared for the showing;
He loaded the carnage and cloaked his dreams with opium.

The local politician pontificated on sacrifices maximum,
His veneration of the value to his voters so much crowing.
His constituents lacked collective condemnation of the forum.
The television tyrannized the teens, its talking heads knowing
That conventional converts coveted courage ad nauseam.

The population politely placed candles and chrysanthemums,
Some conceding concessions for Christ, rote verses flowing.
Both prideful and pretentions patriots composed his requiem.
The pontiff recited rites, a Sanguinem Innocentem for coping…
The family's foundation was fractured once he was forgotten.

At Verde View Nursing Home

The old folks here all seem barely alive.
They barely move, their eyes blank and vacant.
Their spirits seem Earth-bound; they lack all drive.
Each stuck in a cycle where each breath is a pennant.

But in this despair, one old man revives.
His heart is wild, and his words are trenchant.
Ninety-five years now this good war vet has survived,
Though some days he strives to receive his just payment.

To one such as I he has lived many lives.
His stories seem sagas of a true warrior's station.
Once a prisoner of war, he was compelled to connive.
And in these, his golden years, he lives to make a statement.

About the Author

Shannon Fabre is a native of Louisiana who now resides in Colorado. After the birth of her second child, she was diagnosed with Post-Partum Depression Psychosis. These poems are a reflection of that experience.

www.ingramcontent.com/pod-product-compliance
Lightning Source LLC
Chambersburg PA
CBHW031617040426
42452CB00006B/568